Ugly Cute Animals

by Melvin and Gilda Berger

SCHOLASTIC INC.

cover: © Ardea/Thomas Marent/Animals Animals; back cover: © Stephen Dalton/Nature Picture Library; 1: Floridapfe from S.Korea Kim in cherl/Getty Images; 2: © Justin Horrocks/iStockphoto; 3 top right: Jabruson/Naturepl.com; 3 bottom left: Nick Barwick/NPL/Minden Pictures; 4: Life On White/Exactostock/SuperStock; 5 top: Bojana Korach/Oxford Scientific/Getty Images; 5 bottom: Mark Klotz/Getty Images; 6: DC Photo Getty Images; 7 top: Jacqueline Hunkele/Getty Images; 7 bottom: Chris Brignell/FLPA/Minden Pictures; 8: hagit berkovich/Shutterstock; 9 top and bottom: Floridapfe from S.Korea Kim in cherl; 10: Martin Van Lokven/Minden Pictures; 11 top: Zigmund Leszczynski/Animals Animals; 11 bottom: Design Pics/Corey Hochachka; 12: Michael Patricia Fogden/Minden Pictures/National Geographic Creative; 13 top: Michael & Patricia Fogden/Minden Pictures; 13 bottom: Suzi Eszterhas/Nature Picture Library; 14: Adam Jones, Visuals Unlimited, Inc.; 15 top: Ken Griffiths/NHPA/Photoshot; 15: Jurgen & Christine Sohns/FLPA/Biosphoto; 16: Mark Bowler/naturepl.com; 17 top: Radius/Superstock; 17 bottom: iStock/Thinkstock; 18: Anup Shah/Naturepl.com; 19 top: Suzi Eszterhas/Minden Pictures; 19 bottom: Anup Shah/NPL/Minden Pictures; 20: Jane Burton/Naturepl.com; 21 top: Nature Production/Naturepl.com; 21 bottom: Samuel Dhier/Biosphoto; 22: Mark Newman/Science Source; 23 top: Sylvain Cordier/Biosphoto; 23 bottom: Konrad Wothe/Minden Pictures; 24: John Downer/naturepl.com; 25 top: Mauritius/Photoshot; 25 bottom: Richard du Toit/Gallo Images/Getty Images; 26: Mike Parry/Minden Pictures; 27 top: Oxford Scientific/Getty Images; 27 bottom: David Fleetham/Visuals Unlimited, Inc.; 28: Imagebroker.net/Photoshot; 29 top: Nigel J. Dennis/NHPA/Photoshot; 29 bottom: Solvin Zankl/Minden Pictures; 30: © Torbjörn Arvidson/Robert Matton AB/Alamy; 31 top: Wim Weenink/Foto Natura/Minden Pictures; 31 bottom: Robert Eastman/Alamy.

ISBN 978-0-545-60976-0

12 11 10 9 8 7 6 5 4 3 2 1   14 15 16 17 18 19/0

Printed in the U.S.A.   40
First printing, January 2014

Some animals are ugly, like toads. They are lumpy and bumpy. **Other animals are cute, like kittens.** They are soft and cuddly. But did you know that some animals are ugly and cute at the same time?

elephant shrew

These animals may look odd, but they are also lovable. **They are ugly cute!**

axolotl

Bulldog

Bulldogs have flat noses and wrinkled faces that can seem mean and angry. But bulldogs are actually kind and friendly. They like to be around kids, and they make good pets. Most bulldogs would rather sit on your lap than chase a ball!

Bulldogs have broad shoulders and strong legs.

Sphynx Cat

The **Sphynx cat** has no coat and usually no whiskers or eyebrows either! Without fur, some people think this cat looks creepy. But its warm body feels smooth and soft.

Sphynx cats like to cuddle. They often sneak under the covers and sleep with their owners!

Fennec Fox

The **fennec fox** is a small fox with huge ears. Very big ears may look funny on such a small body, but they help this ugly cute animal. Fennec foxes live in the **desert**, where it can get very hot. Its super-big ears give off body heat, which helps the fox keep cool.

Fennec foxes are active at night.

Red-Eyed Tree Frog

The **red-eyed tree frog** has red eyes, a green body, blue-and-yellow sides, and huge orange feet.

These clownish colors may look strange, but they help the frog stay safe. The colors dazzle its enemies. While **predators** stop and stare, the frog hops away!

Sloth

The **sloth** is the slowest **mammal** in the world. It has a coat of long, stringy hair. The sloth's gray coat helps it blend into its home in the trees. Sloths spend most of their time hanging upside down from a branch. They hold on with their arms and legs. A mother sloth gives birth in a tree.

Her belly makes a cozy bed for the baby!

Emu

Emus are huge birds that cannot fly. They have feathery heads and large, staring eyes. Emus are playful animals. On hot days they lie on their backs in the water, kicking their long, thin legs into the air!

Emus have strong legs and good eyesight.

Llama

A **llama** looks like a camel without a hump. Many have banana-shaped ears and bad manners. Llamas are very strong so people use them to carry heavy loads. Sometimes they get tired, hot, and angry. They spit and kick and act **stubborn**. But who can resist their warm eyes and long eyelashes?

Orangutan

Orangutans are large apes with very long arms. Their bodies are covered with a coat of messy reddish hair. When they stand, their fingertips almost touch the ground. Orangutans look fierce, but they are actually very gentle.

Female orangutans make excellent moms!

Axolotl

The **axolotl** is a type of salamander that spends its life underwater. It walks along lake bottoms on four little feet. It breathes underwater through feathery **gills** that stick way out from its head. It has no **scales** or hair.

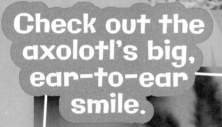

Check out the
axolotl's big,
ear-to-ear
smile.

Okapi

The **okapi** is one very mixed-up animal. It has the legs of a zebra, the body of a horse, the ears of a deer, and the head of a giraffe!

But its long, purple tongue is far stranger than any other part of its body. Its tongue is so long that the okapi uses it to wash its face—and even clean its ears!

Elephant Shrew

The **elephant shrew** is the size of a mouse, with a tiny **trunk** like that of an elephant! All day, it pokes its elephant-like nose under leaves on the forest floor, looking for food.

The elephant shrew sticks its tongue out beyond the end of its trunk. Flick! It grabs a bug for dinner!

Elephant shrews eat spiders, centipedes, and earthworms.

Dugong

The **dugong** is a large mammal that lives in the sea. Up close, it looks big and clumsy. Its mouth is on the bottom of its head to let it eat sea grass on the ocean floor. But from far away, dugongs do not look gawky at all. They seem graceful and almost human.

Sailors used to think dugongs were mermaids!

Meerkat

Meerkats sleep in crowded tunnels that they dig with their two front feet. By day, they come up out of the tunnels to search for food. Standing on their strong back legs, they warm their bellies in the sun. They also take turns babysitting and watching out for predators.

Meerkats stand guard and bark or whistle if they spot danger.

Hedgehog

The ugly cute **hedgehog** is covered with sharp **quills**. It got its name because it looks for food in hedges and grunts like a hog or pig. When in danger, the hedgehog rolls itself into a prickly ball to protect itself from predators!

GLOSSARY

Desert – A dry area with little rain and few plants.

Gills – The parts of an animal that let it breathe underwater.

Mammal – A warm-blooded animal with a backbone that nurses its offspring.

Predators – Animals that hunt other animals for food.

Quills – Stiff, pointed hairs that completely cover some animals.

Scales – Bits of hard material that cover the outside of some animals.

Stubborn – Not willing to give in or change.

Trunk – The long nose of an animal.